The Calendar of Heresies

by

M. C. Rush

Copyright© 2023 M. C. Rush
ISBN: 978-93-95224-55-0

First Edition: 2023
Rs. 200/-

Cyberwit.net
HIG 45 Kaushambi Kunj, Kalindipuram
Allahabad - 211011 (U.P.) India
http://www.cyberwit.net
Tel: +(91) 9415091004
E-mail: info@cyberwit.net

No part of this book may be reproduced or transmitted in any form or by any means, electronic, mechanical, photocopying, or otherwise, without the express written consent of M. C. Rush.

Printed at VCORE.

Acknowledgments

I would like to thank the editors of the following journals and websites for first publishing some of the poems collected here.

Spinebind: "A Window"

The Hamilton Stone Review: "Necronyms"

The Legendary: "Lingering," "Modus Operandi"

World is suddener than we fancy it.
World is crazier and more of it than we think...

—Louis MacNeice
from "Snow"

Today, I have learned
That to become
A great, cracked,
Wide-open door
Into nowhere
Is wisdom.

—May Sarton,
from "Of the Muse"

Contents

Wordeal 9
Variation on a Theme of Variation on a Theme 10
The Snake, and the Apple, and the Fig Leaf 11
Our Words 12
The Protocols of Change 13
Connoisseurs of Truth 14
Hope Got Loose 15
What I Have To Say 16
For What Error, This Penalty? 17
The Annals 18
What Is Meta For? 19
Any Time 20
"The Desperate Exercise of Failing Power" (T. S. Eliot) 21
Looking Back 23
On the Nature of Things 24
Neosphere 25
La chasse au bonheur 26
Beautiful Warnings 27
The Life Squads 28
Calabobos 29
Acquisition 30
Voyeur 2 31
I Heard It Somewhere Said 34
Persistence Song 35
The Lovely Lonely Bones of Hand and Home 36
Yugen 37
Riddle of the Sphinxter 38
Exogamy 39
Nothing 40
Contemplation 41
Psychomanteum 42

The Mythology of Prey Animals	43
Necronyms	44
Anxiety 2	45
Across the Line	46
Draft	47
Apotheosis	48
Sea Chantey	49
Assuming the Position	50
Epiphyte	51
The Calendar of Heresies	52
A True Story That I Made Up	53
A Deep Hole	54
Something Else	55
What's Left	56
Modal	57
Halloween Poem	58
Desire's Song	59
Foreclosure	60
Hullabaloo	61
The Impulse	62
I Want To Write Like The Sea Writes	63
The Evidence	64
Acedia	65
The Heritage World and the Choosing Moon	66
The Boast	68
Lingering	69
Lost in the Libyrinthary	70
Motes	71
The Programming	72
I Think I Thought	73
Ubiquity	74
The Constituency	76
El Roto	77
The Joke	79
Etiology	80

Modus Operandi	81
A Window	82
Thanatopsis	83
The Evidence 3	84
Skullmusic	85
In The Duller Realms	86
Bent	87
Mundungus	88
Sympathetic Noise	89
The League of Intention vs. the Federation of Result	90
Panopticon	91
The Moment	92
Let's Say	94
Pentriloquism	95
Bonfire of the Inanities	96
Less So	97
Someone For Everyone	98
Disappearing	99
Tomorrow Mourning	100
Too Short	101
When I Think	102
This Side of the Grass	103
The Predations	104
Audience	105
Philosophy at 760 Miles/Hour	106
Let There Be Time	107

Wordeal

Give me a sea ten years unfished,
a forest fifty years unhunted,
two hundred years unlogged.
Let me sleep deep in a deep cave
till the whole world is restored by neglect.

The difference between a long time and forever,
the same as the difference between a moment and forever.

How much supernatural survives the death of death?
Is there any error more common than the assumption of necessity?
The rupture of conjecture, parallax from the belvedere's
apoplexiglass, parabiosis, that appetite that's shaped the world
to be less receptive, every birth, another wound.

If the eternal is infernal
then condemn me now forever.

Variation on a Theme of Variation on a Theme

everything that I have taken in
(or been taken in by) in this
life

particle, wave, expectation,
extrapolation, wish

the interplay of the uncertain
producing conjunctions of reality,
ephemeral, essential

existence without description,
unique combinations of sameness,
extravagance without waste

the difference between what there was
and what we thought there was

consolidated consolations

The Snake, and the Apple, and the Fig Leaf

Tradition is a bubble of history waiting to pop.

I need this world,
but I need worlds that don't contain this world
and which aren't contained by it.

We're not the descendants of Adam and Eve, obviously,
but of the snake, and the apple, and the fig leaf.
Of the story.

Your words are not yours, my words not mine.
We use them like idlers playing checkers
with the wriggling carapaces of insects.

Words are sublimated violence,
excrementitious threats and promises
tuned for acquisition. Sometimes.

There are better things to put in the void than prayers.

Our Words

Using our words to separate and sort
the cerebral vantage of my song,
the carnal savage of my soul,
taking all the pieces from which others
produce the world and making something else
(who says the awkward cadence is dishonest?
that lies can't rhyme?),
small mound of achievement
under shadow of the mountain of loss,

and now no one can bear
to proposition chance—
play it cool play it safe
play it to win—
I fall upon the neck of life, I need.

The Protocols of Change

anyone could be harboring anything
at any time thoughts hopes intent
we must turn them all inside out
turn ourselves inside out show how
serious we are about our innocence
and how damned hard we work all the time
to take a lot but keep so little inside that
we are lightened by every acquisition
that we give back everything that we borrow
slightly changed from how we found it
and all we retain from moment to moment
are the protocols of change
and the mechanisms of whim

Connoisseurs of Truth

C'est le mot qui me soutient
— Aimé Césaire, from "Barbare"

the links are play, the connections are a game,
the truth is loose

finally tiring of it, at last becoming too tired
to continue looking everywhere, at everyone,
for hints, for answers to my own questions, which I
assumed (rightly, I still think) were everyone's questions

but if I don't teach you something
or you don't teach me something
what will become of us?

we have two eyes
the one that looks at
and the one that looks away

when our games become sophisticated enough
that we can believe them without reservation
then human desire shall at last be requited

Hope Got Loose

Hope got loose
and threatened to overwhelm a universe
content with cause and effect,

and so it responded with Life,
an immune reaction which went right to work,
destroying the interloper

by grabbing on and not letting go,
by inflating it with the breath of kisses,
by infecting it with seeds of need.

What I Have To Say

what I have to say
I have to say what
others have said what
I have heard what
I could hear

so hear me now
while I say again what's
been said before so
you hear again what
lives in echo

For What Error, This Penalty?

the unimaginable is unchangeable;
the unimagined is a challenge

the two kinds of extravagance
with the formal optimism of *good morning*

the stories of power
vs. the power of stories

from in out
from out in

approximation, not precision;
"good enough," not right

not all intricacy is exaggeration,
nor exquisite

beware the crafty liar
who always tells the truth

a different sample will come to you
than the sample you go and collect

everything matters
though it may not matter to you

rehearsals of acceptance,
still refusals

The Annals

[Pessimissimo]

Feed too much to too many and the
annals of the hero-villain will make room.
The best fool is the sentimental fool.
'Tis but the best of all possible worms.
Hate speech is love speech misspoken.
To decide for the side of those who decide,
the sacred massacred, the laying down of arms,
the lying down for love, or death, hokey-but-legit,
how we make such complexity out of so many
simple things, out of the naive belief in the unfinished.
Our undeclared devotions resist taxation.
The bliss of the curse of partial knowledge.
Half our time is spent trivializing half
the other half.

What Is Meta For?

Vanquishing evil is noble, but it is not enough. I take an impression of everything, looking for the key. Looking for the cautious dissonance in harmony. Looking for incarnations of incantation. There's my interest in X. My fascination with Y. My obsession with Z. Looking to accept the adequacy of accuracy. Of inaccuracy. Preliminary analysis. Preliminary estimate. Preliminary. Invention or discovery? Lyre or lucre? Tell me something. Sentient sentences. Sacrifice is a penurious exchange. Looking for inevitability in chaos, sanity in madness. That sounds good. Looking for compassion for the clueless, promoting all the martyrologies of those eager to make everything unspeakable. As the descriptive devolves into the derogatory. On some level even a condemnation is a celebration. Right? Name it and they will make it. The murmur of the colloquium. The opposite of obscure is obscene.

Any Time

a population of alchemists
seeking to transmute life into ash

we who have outsourced our wars
our loves our lives
shall rejoice at our profit
which surely shall arrive
at any time

similar components
endlessly remixed
amidst pockets of absence
almost visible
in the continuum
of expectation

ripening into rot

"The Desperate Exercise of Failing Power" (*T. S. Eliot*)

Are we so unwilling that the world should outlast us
that we've taken it upon ourselves to see that it doesn't?
What can we deduce about the world
from a study of the evolved traits of its creatures?
(Variation may seem to imply creation,
but it's only change plus time.)
The first species we domesticated—us.

Glittersnipes afraid to disbelieve the lie inside,
lacking the capacity for complexity, settling for complication,
not playful enough, not childlike enough, not serious enough,
neurotraumatized by an impromptu romp, confounded
by asymmetrical notions of lewdness, by words
destabilized by the endless onslaught of their connotations—

*we need a punctuation mark that speeds up words—
all ours slow and hinder them—*

would-be oracles of opacity, straining toward autism,
their names, the least interesting thing about them.
But still interesting.

No matter how much beauty is destroyed, *ultra vires*,
we will always find more, consume it, voracious and careless,
to cultivate a boredom not susceptible to manufactured drama
in the tradition of killing an old god to make a new world without
questioning the provenance of the parts used to construct each
    Frankenself,

uniformity producing variance, unpropitious ambition, interference from the clash of agendas with the precision of persuasion. (You will exhaust yourself long before you will exhaust life.)

That which can be hidden is incidental.
There's a time for holding on and a time for moving on.
We need more time to grow apart from others.
From the disquieting comfort of the mirrors and funnels of proximal tradition.
Sleep without waking would not be sleep.

Looking Back

How shall we organize our emptiness?
See. See. See.

There is no copying of form without distortion.
Meaning overcomes this.

What we look for looking back are fragments of today,
to proceed with a density of purpose

existing only in the the emergination.
The pretense of simplicity, the pose of natural array.

Imagine a world where we are all the same
and determined to believe we are different.

On the Nature of Things

Our source matters, of course, but our angles
of diffraction, our scatter, matter more.

Progress is a slightly, but significantly, less
preposterous repository for faith than religion.

The more you concentrate on what is,
the more you are confronted with what isn't.

The knownothingness of certainty.

That the world veers so from expectation
is its saving grace.

Paradise imagined
is paradise lost.

Begin to constrict
and you will end obstructed.

Harmony requires deviance.

Neosphere

Some leaves are fingers and some are faces.

Error never goes extinct,
for the desperate, wooed from worship,
rescued from the senseless
by promise of significance,
by pledge that alleged love will materialize
in material things, in justice,
in fortune struck by luck,
in being embraced (if blindly) by the mistaken,
the confused, and the lost,
pursue the music of affinities
juxtaposed with transient uncertainties.

Nature says it's easier to make
more of a thing than to protect it.

La chasse au bonheur

If you were to drag a gravestone through a carnival,
would you choose styrofoam or granite?

There are so many more answers than there are questions
(and there are so many questions!).

Dreaming is not a process separate from consciousness.
Rain doesn't obscure as much as clouds do.

When you interrogate me
when you are alone
how inadequate are my answers?

The presence of pestilence,
the absence of diagnosis.

The disappointing thing about nature
is her lack of humor.

Beautiful Warnings

that experience cripples expectation,
that narrative is condescending,
the didactic query, inquiry through assertion,
things carefully said or carelessly said,
the fundamental utterance,
the incantation of intention,
diverse claims, aims, and standards,
the obsession with conflict, beautiful warnings,
the administration of conclusion, contingency
plans and other dreams, the productivity
of consumption, the terror of being measured
by our possessions, the pathology of organization,
the rhetoric of non-tactical connections, perversion
of preference, the appeal of the appalling,
the liking of like minds, the difference between
what can be done, what you can do,
getting things done or getting things right,
the weakness-seeking attention of erosion,
the banality of the soul

the vital power we lack is erasure,
there is no "nature,"
only tendencies

The Life Squads

There is no special abomination
only general horror
so deploy the life squads
the curious and the cautious
marked marred married
made of the depraved
privations of living to eliminate
the miserable mysteries
of sated minds mentored
by meteors to gather
the opportunistic harvest
of inopportune moments.

There is no luck, only chance,
and chance is entirely dependent
upon circumstance.

In hell, or in heaven, when able,
one should condemn what's inevitable.

Calabobos

part shadow
part post-prism light
facets blur curve
part movement
part never-has-moved

The source is never tainted,
the channels of delivery, always.
Choices are never entirely ours.

Thirsty dowsers, following our rods
here and there and here again
seeking an out from this world of drought.

Possibilities,
prophet-seized,
skeptic-freed.

That delight at discovering someone's reality.
Not quite a door, not exactly a window.
The way to break time is to stage adjacency.

The hidden, the undiscovered, are delicious;
the inaccessible is not to my taste.
Viability is always valuable.

Acquisition

From desire, dissatisfaction...
but also acquisition.

Don't stretch decency to preference.
It's not selfish to want more.

What responsibility do we bear for the impoverished universe
that provided conditions for us to develop want and little else?

If there is no moral justification for taking,
then moral life is impossible.

If all life is inherently amoral,
then what use can life make of moral theory?

One can want, one can consume,
without proceeding directly to gluttony.

Another word for sated
is invalidated.

Voyeur 2

I.

peeping at every little pip of life
like Tom: amazed, aghast, attracted

what do voyeurs see that others don't?
what do spies know that others can't?

what are humans when abstracted
and stripped of the impulse to hide?

have what you can't have
know what you don't know

all for one or one for all?
or each to each, to watch, to own?

II.

in the desert
I saw so little
even of myself,
could hardly calm sound
into silence

III.

value isn't inherent, but dependent

no, that isn't it—like Schrödinger's cat,
it capitulates to reality when you look at it

IV.

don't look
if you don't want to act

V.

seeing is
  a) believing
  b) deceiving
  c) grieving

VI.

watching others for their moments
of weakness that could conceivably be
my openings, entries, gaps to trap
their yeses and trip their nos
so as to see how much of me
they'd see through the acid seas
of their eyes—I'm no prize
to arise from the trash—but I don't
bother, it'd be intrusive, and rash,

and I fear the tears of strangers
who rearrange their messes
to accommodate my intrusion
or even my approach

      VII.

see the comforting murmurs of poetry
see the discomfiting murmurs of poetry

I Heard It Somewhere Said

This damned Stone, transmuting all my similes
to observations of difference, measures of unlikeness.

Tell the slant but tell it true.
How much variation to change from same?

Use categories where they are useful,
but never, ever trust them.

Subjectivity is localized modeling.
Include internondependencies.

Not everything is sex madness.
There is also regret.

Never let them force you to choose
between flavor and nutrition.

Our weakest power is rejection,
yet we use it like it were our greatest strength.

Persistence Song

A cunning culling
of seeming sense
from the rest.

The layers of time
made of everything
except acceptance.

Do we judge the affinity of water for water,
blame the poles of a magnet for their attractions
and repulsions?

My brain, a representative
democracy, failing, desperately
electing more representatives.

Sure, we are irreparable,
but the breaking is bearable
so long as there is growth.

The joys discovered in difficulty
are unexpected, and unrepeatable.
Inexhaustible.

The Lovely Lonely Bones of Hand and Home

an obsolescent
anointing the arcane, the insane, and the inane
with inconsistent consent

potential
held in escrow

liminal energy
locked up in litigation

the *koi no yokan*
in every mirror

intimacy being extrinsic
daysung nightwhispers

what proxy can suffice
when you can't be
where you need to be?

Yugen

Addicted to cinematic revelation, parallel
parables more recognition than recall,
more water than wind, more wash than push,
I seek seclusion like water recedes down a crevice.

How much you interfere with other people's
storylines determines your level of villainy.

The dog isn't smelling the flower,
he's smelling the mysterious urine on the flower.
Gilded by the ornament of dissent?
Or guided by its insistence on sense?

Anonymous is not synonymous
with incognito.

Fog is more honest
than the clearest reflection
in the most well-meaning puddle.
Precedence doesn't guarantee primacy.

Riddle of the Sphinxter

Liberty—Fraternity—Technology,
intricate delicacies, jolly folly:
an epidemic of epic contortions;

Pepper's ghost, poltergeisty,
panning political theater (often awful)
to feel a gleemer among the seemiliar;

diatomaceous text, contrasting
priorities, improvident suppositions,
the anxiety of emphasis;

life thriving then crashing on excess, dreams
of sensual clarity, postbiotic cognitive eroticism
calculating assets midst cloistered carnage

forever and after.

Exogamy

Who's the catalyst and who's the cause?
Who fissiparous? Melting's not leaking.

I doubt the I
remembering the memories.

The suspicion that description misses essence.
Your words, your least persuasive emanation.

What I am
questions what you are
where it differs from what you are.

Give me the stormlight, the twilight, the dusk.

I can do what doesn't need doing
but I'd rather watch you.

How did you know? What gave me away?
I don't think I have to answer that to answer that.

Nothing

The exactly-right detail
shows nothing,
the exactly-right word
says nothing,
the exactly-right connection
links nothing
without something
to approximate experience,
to say everything means,
to see everything matters.

Contemplation

Nothing cannot exist.
Can it not-exist?
How constrained existence is!
And it is everything.
Even the seems-to-exist-but-doesn't
exists conceptually.
Nothing cannot exist
without becoming something,
so nothing cannot exist.
Yet we think of it,
so it exists in our thoughts.
We speak of it,
so it exists in our speech.
In the something we make of nothing
in order to know it,
in order to point at it.
Because nothing cannot exist.

Psychomanteum

tasteful
pride-empty
spaces

storm cellar
undermound bunker
bomb shelter
panic room

maya is maya
oursourced

revelation reveals
only
glimpses of self

surfing the sea of fear,
sinking, surfacing

intimidating infinity
with intangible aspiration

vanity is the seventh desperation

The Mythology of Prey Animals

convergence of convenience
caricature of caring

to freshen up
with a weeping

infinite egress
inauthentic eccentric

senses not functions
assimulated

to thrive eternally
the secret please

inconsistent consent
earning regret

to remember remembering
but forgetting forget

Necronyms

The silence that isn't silence
is a cacophony of self
echoing in the cocoon.

All of our names for everything are wrong.
Because they're ours and all things
have better names of their own.

Not a rejection, just a recognition.
How better to destroy something
than by discovering its name?

Everything means,
though it may not mean to me.
Poetry, poverty. Many, one.

How better to discover something
than by destroying its name?
Garish description of rococo perception.

Shy electrons,
energy, enemy,
fouled with fame.

Anxiety 2

We won't know what to do
until we see what we are.

Cold in the skin
but warm at the core.

If repetition is the enemy of joy,
we must change everything always.

We are expected to bring
more than we find.

What is wasted in one place, position, or time
may be revered in another.

How far can we go
resisting loss?

Which matters more,
truth, or access to truth?

Across the Line

A little ink more or less!
It surely can't matter? —Stephen Crane

How many places do we arrive at
that the thing we need has just departed from
or not yet come to?

\<put yourself here\>

Love is not love without a lack of love,
a flaw in the lover that acknowledges
the flaw in the loved.

\<put your love here\>

Some just know (or know of) complexity
and some don't.
Communication is hard across the line.

\<put your loss here\>

How many whispers
do we miss
midst all the yelling?

Draft

I don't like lies
but artifice is nice

what you think about
what you think

aphasic oracles
stop posing your questions either/or

trust your voices
to find the words you need

no time to come to terms with anything
no terms to come to anything with time

what you think about
what you think about

don't pretend inevitability
where chance will do

Apotheosis

Such a boring chore
to decide which frustrates more:
denial or indifference!

Intoxicated modes of endurance:
joy midst desolation;
production in ruin;
generosity in deprivation.

Lusty shouts
will keep you deaf
to immoral whispers.

There is no vantage
that reveals the entire battle.

You were strong in your moment of weakness,
now you'd be weak in your moment of strength?

Sea Chantey

brine brink
vast void

arid groove
under putrid curl

wave wherein
splash sang
to cherish extravagance

all the dead unknown
unfurled
dropped ashore

to collect and stink
on abandoned beach

or hidden in
the convenient deep

Assuming the Position

Non deceptus est qui scit se deceptum.

our finite bit of the infinite
only whets our appetite

lessening lessons into learning
imagining affirmations in traffic sounds in sirens
in diesel exhaust spilled beer spoiled food
in money in friendship in love

in each thing every thing all things

to subvert the superficial
the compromises we find beautiful
the imperfect pressings of precedent
the false names of nostalgia

addicted to existence

I stand with the others
between me and the truth

Epiphyte

Subversive automata,
ergonomic, erogenous,

seeking machine-assisted nirvana
among the probable problems.

Noble
or merely notable.

Theft to gift.
Love was made.

I'm not saying anything.
I'm doing something.

To define without negative connotation
all of our terms.

To deny doctrine is to deny heresy.
This is the way that I feel.

The Calendar of Heresies

address desire or face desperation
conditions are propitious

the morality of predation
and other haptic relations

the irony of committing ourselves to freedom
ensleeved in temporary flesh sacks

solipsistic shibboleths
marking holidays on the calendar of heresies

the decadence of relishing thrills
swearing dud oaths

the thundering blunders preceding understanding
stoking resentment of the nemesis

if murder is wrong then death is wrong
a just war is just war

A True Story That I Made Up

So originally "clarity" and "enlightenment" were terms for the unique state achieved by volunteers (later "volunteers") who were given a drink of an elixir brewed from the fermented fruit of a now-extinct shrubbery mixed with the powder of a long-neglected local rhizome and the juice of a once-popular mollusc ("*the little dream clam*") which had the effect of rendering them all-but-dead for two days, during which period ceremonial obsidian blades would be used to flense the skin from large areas of their bodies, after which procedure they would be rolled in a specially-prepared mud with a high clay content which would form a thin shell around them. When they would begin to show signs of waking after the second day, the mud coat would be rinsed away with rainwater gathered from natural karst basins and *the Harvested Ones*, as they were known in the regional dialect, would be propped up on a sacred ledge from which they could view the sun and sky over the tropical green of the forest below. The Harvested Ones would often survive from one to three days in this condition, intermittently meditating, singing traditional painsongs, watching, and feeling everything, all over, in an ecstatic posture of unified awareness that others would come and observe during their mandated *visits of gratitude*.

The record of exactly what was done with the skins has been lost in the passage of time.

A Deep Hole

Puzzles are trivial,
mysteries enlist.

Uncertainty *is* reality.
I claim my right to ignore any pretense.

If it cannot change,
it can't exist.

If we only exist in our attention
we can only be a speck in infinity.

Capacity and solution:
these are everything.

Which is more important, a deep hole
or all that has fallen into it for a thousand years?

How we clutch at our petty compulsions,
anointing them with grace!

Something Else

promiscuous with various scions of empiricism
nothing I can say   fully expresses   what I think

parodying tendencies imperfectly paralyzed in sleep
systemic chaos negated by additional consideration

memory embers
unable to restore
the flame of before
to write on white
with black

opportunity confiscated
by sedated celebrants of heroism of necessity

allowed one motion   one   one at a time
to throw what we hold
or try to catch something else

What's Left

if insects are what's left
of dragon engineering,
what do they compute?

our glance
and the long, locked gaze of the sphinx
scan the same instant
blind with the same intent

the partial perceptions
and apprehensions
that make up our reality
and our illusions

the grave accepts
this one and that
without complaint

Modal

Walking the earth looking for a castle
that has forgotten to maintain its walls,
surrounded by the whisperoar,
the constant almost-threat of the timid fist,
struggling to separate the pain of absence
from the disappointed expectation of presence,
I claim every echo
of every word,
every opportunity to experience and express
various aspects of the model
adapting, diverging, under variable conditions.
We adhere to coherence here, dubbing it fear.

Everything anyone calls unnatural
is as natural as flowers and rain.

Halloween Poem

If you most fear the unknown that lurks in the dark
then you haven't walked long enough in the dark.
What introduces itself has sharper claws and a more savage bite.
Pain is known unseen. Loss is a scream.
Every step you take in the dark moves you closer to disaster.
In the light, too. Standing still makes you even more of a target.
For teeth. So you walk on. Between long rows of pumpkin grins
that go out one by one. This is known. This is seen.
Your fear is the only light left in the dark, so small,
and flickering.

Desire's Song

Shall I acquire you
bit by bit or all at once?
Should I hurry you along
or make you wait?
I don't always want to hint.
Sometimes I want to shout
with excitement
or from disappointment.
It's a hard decision,
approximation or precision.
I'd hate to love too soon
or late. Should I proceed
or call it quits?
Are what the words want
what I want?
Do I need what the words need?

Foreclosure

going every morning to rut
on stone shadowed in the cathedral's dusk,
a place shaped and assembled by the lost,
old when old was new

bare skin spotted by colored shafts of light
alive with motes enough for every eye,
it's on the cold floor we sweat and sigh,
eschewing both altar and pew

our voices joined in heavenly choir
singing again and again our desire,
we kindle among the dead a living fire,
or at least a spark or two

Hullabaloo

Thank you for your repetitions, time-shaped selves,
people in deep cover protecting people in deeper cover,
continuing to conduct presumptive measures of receptivity
along the inevitable trajectory of intimacy, afraid of the sober eye,
the somber mouth, the terrible cherished dream of the inevitable
confounded by coincidence, idioms of convenience,
the iterative efforts of dreams to express
not chaos but infinite canvasses of control.

If anyone
were in charge
the messages
would align.

If a thing is truly lost when its name is lost, why am I
more surprised by senseless noise than senseless action?

The Impulse

man cannot live by word alone

traces of trance
throughout target-rich environments

one vowel, one vow

her smile is like a simile
connecting her to me

citing a study

always choose the one that doesn't make you choose
the impulse to acquiesce

the way her sashay negates my strut

those who want
must never be allowed

enduring is endearing

under the veneer of care

I Want To Write Like The Sea Writes

I want to write like the sea writes:
endlessly, rhythmically, essentially,
influenced only by the moon
and periodic tectonic shift.

There is as much specific in the general
as general in the specific.

Words can do more than provoke pictures!

Learning more and more
until what I learned before
contradicts
and conflicts.

Linear disorder
linking sound to sound—
and back around.

The Evidence

judge someone's philosophy
by its degree of generosity

any examination of the evidence
would force us to conclude
that the intended purpose of life
is to master frustration

to sit on the edge of a sun
tossing in worlds that sink,
never skip, feeding the furnace
the indigestible ejecta of chance,
the ethereal inertia of hope

a fascination with old things
does not preclude a hunger for new

all of my poems are love poems,
for I love the truth

Acedia

how
when what you think you're doing
isn't what you're doing
what you're doing
isn't what you're thinking
isn't
isn't what
isn't what when
what when what
you think

The Heritage World and the Choosing Moon

Not every observation is a complaint, is it?
Fine, I complain.
Better to protect than defend
if you're given a choice.

Hateful people, contemptible people,
I sing and will ever sing against your coal souls,
will never be bullied into appeasing your demands,
or others', that your dreams of rot and violence
be accorded equal standing with growth and kindness,
hope, and tolerance of all but the intolerant.

When love becomes ubiquitous, love becomes useless.

Living with the provisional
through the delusional,
I believe more in the personal
than the political,

in what I put on the plate before I pass it down,
whether I can spare it, whether I share
something vile or my dearest delicacies.
Everything every human has ever done
has been part of a coping strategy,
a hoping strategy, instinctual or intentional.

You insist that I wear a mask,
but what if the world is costumed instead
and I go about with the grace of a naked face?

It takes both the modern and the historic to make the future.
Be the one that opens,
let others come behind bricking it up—
they may be important
but it's not important that you join them.

The Boast

Most forgiveness is forgetting.
Hardness reflects and fragility rejects.
The dream is to make something of nothing,
and each tries in his own way, every day.

To what extent
must diversity include the noncompliant?

Down at Despot Depot
treasure turned cruft
under the affluent influence of
fat toads bellowing a thin din
in the rhythm of the wobble
throughout the long dark nights of the soil
the boast maintains the beast.

Washington crossed the Delaware
and a river never forgives.

Lingering

They blink, they parrot, their eyes nervously seek for
an escape from responsibility, from judgment, from *being*.
The taste of licorice, the taste of brown sugar
lingering in the mouth long after the meal.
I can still hear them hymning under their breath.
Sleep is up and down a staircase.
The older ones moving more slowly
under the additional weight of ghosts.
We love what we don't
know about them.
The secret to having it all
is to acknowledge what is,
and only what takes forever
takes as long as you think it will.

Lost in the Libyrinthary

How many stories are required
to save your life?

Memories have no time in them:
give them sufficient attention
and each is now.

We killed them all and now
wonder why we're alone.

Gravediggers in a forgotten necropolis working
to reify all our metaphors for sex and solitude
in the union of bliss and emptiness,
in artifacts of priceless trash.

Consciousness—
we need more or less.

To flesh, rock, paper seem certain.

Motes

frozen into birth
we thaw till death
as we ravenously consume
the condemned man's meal
slugs hauling human teeth
from where they needed to be
to where they don't
confounded by the moment behind
and the moment ahead
gratitude and blame
yin and yang to the wight of conscience
buying self-indulgences
motes emoting in others' eyes
confusing prediction for prophecy

The Programming

How strange, the power in attributing significance to the insignificant.
How starved we are, to find sustenance in air, deprived of meat.

Always transitioning from this to that, from now to next,
caressing each that, every this in passing like the wind in its mission:

do something, do everything; say anything, say everything;
only a refusal to move, to breathe, to be, is forbidden.

How can you become disoriented when there is no destination in any direction?
There is room in truth for the unlikely, the unexpected, and the undesired.

The first step toward transcending the programming is acknowledging the programming.
What you would have me respect I am content to notice.

I Think I Thought

I think
I thought

I know
I knew

that I
was me

and you
were you

but now
the line

is not
so clear

between what is there
and what is here

Ubiquity

faces saying
I have something better than you have

and

the people of otherwise
sleep with the fetishes

and

autopsy
without curiosity

and

forced to fight
over what won't sustain them

and

they claim the undesirable is inevitable
to justify its ubiquity

and

you will never love anything
like a leaf loves the light

and

if you do only what you must
there is no you

The Constituency

In the shallow you can only see your own reflection,
but many things, some quite unexpected, can lurk in the deep.
Even with the advantage of its vantage there is much the moon
> doesn't see.

Spend some time with me so I can fall out of love with you
as life's parade becomes more military and less Mardi Gras.
Love is just an excuse for the things we do to one another
or an expression of the guilt we feel for doing them.
Memories don't reside where they were made, but in the head.
> And soon,

that moment when life changes from saying hello to things to
> telling them

goodbye, and the unresolvable mysteries of what's left when
> you've left.

To not mean it is a different approach to meaning.
Heaven is an unworthy dream, a stagnant pond in the landscape
> of infinity.

Too many choices is only a problem because we aren't given
> time to choose them all.

How fortunate that the constituency of the dead is denied a vote.

El Roto

The one who broke it
should try to fix it
and if they don't
that means
it means
nothing
to them
it means
nothing
to them

The one who watched it break
felt it
must wait
forever
forever hating
that it means
something
to them
it means
something
to them

What broke
was broken
was broken by
faithlessness
and fear
and
faithlessness and fear
broke it because
it was weak
because it was
weak
and ready
to break

Breaking the one
from the other one
the illusion of time
on the illusion of bond
means nothing
or something
nothing or
something

The Joke

The truth (for it is no secret) of existence
is that everything is aggregate
and I am that good that good I am and
singing against the harmony of the armory,
as mad as the most inapt simile,
the smug lie of archetype
crippled by mythological purity.
To have been, to be, to will be
will be my to do,
the clackery of old bones striving
to do again as they have done
before, before
the chores of existence
challenged so.
Instinct impels upward
though all are found
mountains of bone down,
spinning gold into straw—
good, useful stuff, straw.
The joke is
that we get the joke.

Etiology

There are so many pains
we must be taught to notice.
The cacalescence of experience.
The limits of the literal.
Disillusioned with illusion,
with inessential oblivion,
we arrange for derangement.
To obey authority, to betray autonomy.
Irksome luciferase tears
sharing skin with infinity.
Yesterday is only a lesson.
Tie the hearts that grieve
into concupiscent sheaves.
Love repeals apathy.

Modus Operandi

The law in lieu of love,
the cause of curse, of course.

To assess and accept
immoderate meanings.

Repellant rebellions
still pulse the blood.

The only real connection's
when another's changes change you.

Simmering irritation
in the necessary now.

From emancipated to emaciated,
a brief vibration.

Futile faults, still prejudicial,
of interstitial caricature.

A Window

Perhaps the only thing that belongs to you
is your belief that things are yours.

The illusion of continuity.
The seeming severity of serenity.

The insistence that one choose
a superficial depth or a deep superficiality.

I'm smart enough to know
I'm not smart enough to know.

Everyone wants to sell you the world
while only renting you a place in it.

Our rooms come furnished with fuel,
fueled with furnishings, furbishings.

Give me a large enough window and an enticing view,
and I shall defenestrate the world.

Thanatopsis

Those who know the world, others, and themselves primarily by
   investigation, and
those who know them mostly through hearing and telling stories
   about them.
Those who believe relinquishing moments to be equivalent to
   deleting photos.
Those who see themselves as fundamentally different, and
those who see themselves as basically similar.

Those convinced that doubt devalues.
Those for whom pleasantries are inaccuracies.
Those who need anger to accompany honesty.
Those who have been at the cutting edge of obsession.
Those who invented "innocence" to promote ignorance.
Those who give equal time to error, with predictable results.
Those who feel they should feel, and those who think they should think.
Those who confuse "tough" with "mean" or "kind" for "weak."
Those who rehearse their concession speech.

The Evidence 3

How much of our lives
should we spend trying to justify our lives?

Bones shaking like a rattlesnake,
making that threat.

The ghost of the host
sustained by the attention of others.

To get them to commit to our illusions
or to validate our commitment to them.

The line between
compromise and capitulation.

Made of error,
proceeding according to error.

All the evidence suggests that we are better
equipped to consider than to know.

Skullmusic

Craving order,
celebrating hierarchy.

Anyone can create a spell.
But with fewer each day susceptible to them,
it may be a waste of time.

We embrace what seems to work
and shed the rest and precipitate
from potential into choice
and from complexity into habit.

Who could ever trust
something that comes
and goes
as unpredictably
as love?

In The Duller Realms

They dumbed it down too much.

Approaching life
with decisive derision
in the duller realms
looking at things people want you to look at
doing things people want you to do
learning things people want you to know
oriel proclamations
of darkness and light
collecting naive complexities
from the indignant ignorant
chasing the greased pig of wisdom.

I don't know much about knowing much
but I think it's an interesting subject.

Bent

The world tries everything
to bend us away from truth.
Tries with ambiguous touches,
lies like prophecy
and lies like history.

In times of reversity
we assume the past fixed
to give memory value
and because we want a safe place,
even one we can't reach,
but entropy is there too,
acts there too.

The thing to beware
(but not to entirely avoid)
is the thing standing in
for another thing.
The worst are those falsehoods
thoroughly rejected
yet somehow internalized.

Everything is made of wisps.
Wisdom is a dream,
ignorance is this.

Mundungus

No one forgets.
We just don't remember to remember.
The bucolic perversions of prior generations
building more sewers to remove the excess of success.
A lifetime deducing difference in sameness.
The thing you look back on and regret
is not the same as the thing you enjoyed or suffered
or enjoyed *and* suffered.

Old men and women
dithering over the apocrypha of their lives,
the uncanny valley between young and old
presumably bridged by hope and nostalgia.

Which the more damning,
disappointment or hate?

Sympathetic Noise

hell does not reveal its flames,
it promotes its desperate illusions

adequate evidence
of the constraint of prior choices

pseudo-psyches
ogling the cartoons

to see everything as filters for existence,
to find self in selflessness

confusion between the small you
and the everywhere you-like

speaking faces of breath,
failed smiles

the paparazzi stealing candids of Candide
to document the rest of all possible worlds

The League of Intention vs. the Federation of Result

Prisoners of precedent,
we're made of bees
and full of holes,
pursuing a sourplus of employment,
errors of production vs. errors of perception,
the luxury of weeping, wrestling—loosely—
with the ethics of the urge
to meet atrocity with annihilation,
with the purge of excessive focus.

God is maximum entropy,
and who cares?
Forever echoes
in an empty moment.
Retrograde degradation.

Panopticon

Error also lives where all are certain.

We are constantly cursed
but the only damnation is death.

Dead scripture, live culture.
Hard as Iraq.
Identity idolatry.

We say we want certainty
while we pine for surprise.

The sight of rain.
The sound of rain.
The scent of rain.

Not *will it go*
but *how soon* and *how quickly*.

That which describes does not determine.

The Moment

when you start questioning the necessary
stories that you've told yourself about yourself

and long to return to the world
of all that occurred unseen

distance crossed
challenge met

hardship overcome
difficulty surmounted

all your referents obsolete
and your associations unlinked

seeking the aspect of healing
that's not mere repair

trusting others to do their part
without dictating their role

disregarding actions between factions
adorned with admonishments

unintentional gestures of rejection
spurning the unusual or the unlikely

years spent perfecting
a flat affect

and praise the able and amenable
and the limits of contribution

Let's Say

Let's say you didn't mean to.
Let's say your options were limited.
Let's say you couldn't find another way,
didn't see another choice.
Let's say you did what you felt you had to.
Let's say you did the best you could.
Let's say you didn't know better.
Weren't prepared, weren't ready.
That you were misled, deceived.
And let's say you were confused.
Uncertain. Reluctant, even.
Yes, let's say that.

Pentriloquism

It's not wrong to fiddle while everything burns,
only to wait for the flames to start.

Collecting datapoints like a magpie, a packrat
for the ineffectual recreations of memory.

What is overlooked, what is considered,
what is dismissed.

Scorn as a tool,
not an indulgence.

Is all this
so I can speak?

My voice is color,
but my *thoughts* are fire.

How are we to be restored
with freshness banished?

Bonfire of the Inanities

Who can be the same
when everything you want is in front of you
as when everything you want lies behind?

There must be some room
for passion of wanting
alongside desperation of need.

Shall we kill what frightens us
until there is nothing left,
only us, and fear?

So determined that *something* should come
of our having lived that we sponsor destruction
with only the smallest inclination.

Comfort, pleasure
come in series,
don't stay in stasis.

Shall we promote easy parodies of sanity
produced endlessly for purposes
deliquescent?

We must use these moments
to do every little thing.
Or leave them in the infinity of the undone.

Which is the truer memory:
the world saying *Welcome*
or the world saying *You again?*

Less So

What does meaning mean?
Why care about anything but caring about?

When they ask *what did you expect*,
always reply *more and better*.

Too often, living reshuffles character,
weakening one's hand.

I'm okay with *I don't know where I'm going*,
less so with *I don't know where I've been*.

Remember that I was never the man I might have become—
the cloud that doesn't form has promised no rain.

Which yet-to-be me will be the one
to stop letting me down?

Those who exceed their expectations
didn't expect to.

Someone For Everyone

There is a stone made just for you,
a stone
of a certain size and a particular weight
somewhere
among the other stones and sands and soils
of the earth
in a valley, under a field, on a mountainside,
deep down
under fathoms of sea, in a mine, in a canyon,
in a quarry,
within the boundaries of one of the many nations
recently drawn on maps,

igneous, metamorphic, or sedimentary,
magma-made or crashed from space,
this stone, this unique and perfect stone,
it waits, it waits and waits its weight,
waits to be sought, waits to be known,
waits unknown, alone, your stone, so like
and so unlike so many other stones,
all the other stones,
one of which will have to do
to mark the grave
you never looked for
but anyway found.

Disappearing

I am disappearing:
a species' last member, lost;
a mirage, shadowed;
the dew, overstayed till midday;
a dream, alarmed;
a temporary arrangement, no longer agreeable;
a word or sentence, reordered;
a babble, evaporated;
a minute, counted out;
a hunger, fed;
a world, to a closing eye;
a mystery, solved.

Tomorrow Mourning

I shall rise tomorrow mourning
— a name not spoken — a whole left broken —
longing to breakfast.

All day I shall hold my breath.

I shall retire tomorrow mourning
— another day away — another night I lay
my dreams upon the past.

Too Short

and I go on believing things matter
that don't matter

\<and here is a list of things you love\>

what you led me to believe, I don't believe
what you wanted to show me, I don't see
what you meant to give me, I don't have

\<and here a list of things you don't love\>

I can't bear to see you
seeing what you can't bear to see

as ashamed of yourself
as if every person in the world were you

\<and here a list, too short, of what loves you\>

and I will go on believing
things matter that don't matter

\<and here is the world that loves you not\>

endings are insufficient

When I Think

when I think how much has died so I could live
when I think
when I think much how much
how much is dead
now
now I think
oh
now I think
no
but oh yes
and more death has made me
kept and sustained me
than my death will ever give
ever let live

This Side of the Grass

Everyone is a war
for which death buries the casualties.

No one should die for anything
as ephemeral as a belief
or as biased as a conviction.

Is it not enough that we have to
be disappointed by our death?
Do we have to be embarrassed by it too?

I would like time to prepare for mine—
not a welcome, but a proper rebuff.
To ready myself to stare it down
as if it could be shamed
as it deletes me, defeats me.

If you are doing good you're doing well.

The Predations

You know with imprecision
what so many don't know at all—
who is better off?

The predations of mouse and moth
evoke terror because of their number,
not their ardor.

Every day is Judgment Day.
And you're the judge.

George Washington playing Russian roulette
with Gavrilo Princip and Salvador Dali.

When things as large as the sea are dying
how seriously can we take minor matters?
Or do minor matters become the only things
we *can* take seriously?

The end is there, at last.
The end is there, at least.

Audience

The dog watches me to see what I will do.
The dog is dead.
The girl watches me to see what I want.
The girl is gone.
The dream watches me to see what I am.
The dream fades.
The past watches me to see what I can be.
The past miscalculated.
The future doesn't watch me.
The future forgot.

Philosophy at 760 Miles/Hour

Acknowledge what you see.
Admit what you don't.

Label everything
if you hope to win.

Question every label
if you hope to know.

Money is the carrot.
Money is the stick.

No time for review,
all one can do is next.

The thing is to try.
I don't know why,
but the thing is to try.

Let There Be Time

Let there be time,
and days of rest,
and mouths that sing,
and ears that listen.
Let there be time
for movement and change
and transformation
and revolution.
Let there be time
for denial and acceptance,
rejection and embrace,
and for reassessment.
Let there be time for every thing.
Oh, let there be time!

Made in the USA
Columbia, SC
31 January 2023